A HISTORY OF THE
SHAFFER HOTEL

TABLE OF CONTENTS

DEDICATION

I want to dedicate this book to the memory of Clem and Lena Shaffer. They contributed much to the early years of Mountainair's history and were an integral part of making the town a success. The history of Mountainair would not have been the same if Clem and Lena had lived somewhere else and never built and operated the Shaffer Hotel.

PREFACE

MOUNTAINAIR CIRCA 1920s

Shortly after the turn of the twentieth century, the Atchison, Topeka & Santa Fe Railroad established the railroad line known as the Belen Cutoff. Mountainair, founded in 1903, became the first incorporated town in Torrance County. The town quickly developed into a thriving, farming community and was known as the Pinto Bean Capital of the World during its heyday.

Soon a railroad depot, mercantile stores, bean elevators, movie theaters, an elementary and high school and much more were built in the booming community. The town continued to grow as the wet years continued and farmers flocked to the Estancia Valley.

MOUNTAINAIR TRADING COMPANY

The Mountainair Trading Company established in 1917 soon had the biggest store and bean elevator in town. The Company opened in 1918 and closed in 1945. The bean elevators and trucks bringing pinto beans to be processed caused a bustling farming atmosphere in the community when farmers came into town from all parts of the county on Saturday mornings. The women shopped and enjoyed being together while the men visited about crops and the weather. The Pinto Bean Parade was the high point of the year where a Pinto Bean Queen was crowned and the evening ended with a dance. The farmers worked hard, and they enjoyed dancing and having a good time.

SATURDAY IN MOUNTAINAIR
WEAVER COLLECTION
CIRCA 1920s

At the height of the pinto bean era over thirty million pounds of pinto beans were shipped from bean elevators in Mountainair each year. As more people homesteaded and the wet years continued the amount of pinto beans produced tripled between the years of 1916 and 1921. The virgin soil was conducive to pinto bean farming and soon homesteaders were raising it as their main crop.

In 1901, Colonel E.C. Manning arrived in New Mexico Territory with the intent of locating towns along the proposed Belen Cutoff route. The location that would become Mountainair was named after the fresh mountain breezes coming off the nearby Manzano Mountains.

Soon, a railroad depot was constructed near the tracks and homesteaders and settlers flocked to the area. Bean elevators and mercantile stores appeared on Mountainair's Main Street and the town was on its way.

MOUNTAINAIR DEPOT
CIRCA 1910

John Corbett, one of the incorporators of Mountainair, was instrumental in the founding of the town in 1903. He persuaded the Chautauqua Assembly to come to New Mexico, and

Mountainair would hold the first Chautauqua Assembly in the state in August of 1908. Between the years of 1908 and 1917, Mountainair's Chautauqua Park was known throughout the Southwest as a cultural center. Hundreds of visitors traveled long distances each August to attend a ten-day agenda of events consisting of lectures, musical presentations, workshops and more. Camping facilities, a large assembly hall, a lodge and dining room were built for those attending the Chautauqua.

The idea for a Chautauqua was created in 1874 at Chautauqua Lake in New York by Methodist minister, John Vincent. It began as a summer training program for Methodist Sunday school teachers, but quickly expanded into a nation-wide program where lecturers, musicians and artists traveled from one Chautauqua Camp to another and entertained crowds of people camping at the site for their yearly vacation. By 1917, the Chautauqua movement was in decline and did not continue. It was also the year of John Corbett's death.

The Chautauqua movement did a lot to publicize Mountainair's location. During this time, many people migrated to the Mountainair area because they wanted to enjoy a little culture.

JOHN CORBETT

The town continued to develop and grow in the 1920s. With the construction of Pop Shaffer's hotel, the town took on a more civilized atmosphere. More and more homesteaders moved to the area until the rains stopped in the 1930s and it was impossible to grow pinto beans as had been done in the past. Many had to move in order to make a living.

Since Mountainair's pinto bean growing heyday years, the town has lost businesses and population but continues to thrive as a tourist and artist community on the edge of the Manzano Mountains. Artists and retirees have relocated to the old railroad town, and many of the original buildings have been renovated and are once again in use adding life and activity to the town.

EARLY PHOTOS OF
MOUNTAINAIR

Street Scene - Mountainair, New Mexico

Main Street Mountainair, N.M. "Dale Photo"

High School, Mountainair, N. Mex.

CHAPTER ONE --HISTORY OF THE SHAFFER HOTEL

The Shaffer Hotel has been a New Mexico landmark since it was constructed in 1923 during the town's boom years. Mountainair, founded in 1903, was an up and coming town along the Santa Fe Railroad line. The area had filled with pinto bean farmers and Clem Shaffer's Hotel added a sense of civilization to the unsettled country and soon became a destination point for those traveling in the isolated landscape.

ORIGINAL HOTEL SHAFFER 1920s

Pop Shaffer was quite the character according to those who knew him. He enjoyed a drink or two and was constantly trading land or wagons or any item he could find to trade. It seemed he was always involved in some business deal. He enjoyed telling and playing jokes on his friends and was considered a playboy and womanizer. He was never without a cigar in his mouth and he enjoyed fishing and working on his animal art. Shaffer also helped to organize Mountainair's first Fourth of July celebration and played a cornet in the local marching band. He was an active member of the Elks' Club.

Clem Shaffer pushed for the development and success of Mountainair and attempted luring visitors to the Shaffer Hotel and Rancho Bonito south of town. He told wonderful stories about the area and invited people to stay at his ranch. He publicized his ranch with small billboards along the highway leading into town.

Shaffer was born in Harmony, Indiana in 1880. He attended school until he was thirteen years old and then dropped out to learn the blacksmith trade from his father. He was considered a hard worker, but he still found time to court Pearl Brown who lived six miles from Harmony on a farm. Pearl agreed to marry him in 1902 and they had two children named Donald and Mildred.

Later, the small family moved to Lawton, Oklahoma where Clem supported the family as a carriage and buggy painter. The business was flourishing until a tornado ripped through the town destroying Shaffer's home and business. By 1908, Clem and his family had migrated to Mountainair in New Mexico Territory, where he went into the blacksmith business. They struggled to survive on the four dollars a week Pearl made selling butter. Pearl had never been in good health and she succumbed to pneumonia in 1911 leaving Clem to raise their two children.

Clem had always been good friends with Dad Imboden another Mountainair pioneer who homesteaded land north of Mountainair. He was a well respected member of the community. When Pearl passed away, Pop was so upset over her death that he threatened to shoot the doctor who had failed to save her. Dad Imboden talked him out of receiving a murder charge and later his daughter Lena would marry Shaffer.

From most reports, Pop Shaffer was determined to kill the doctor who he felt had allowed his wife to die. Dad Imboden loaned him the money to take Pearl's body back to Indiana and he was gone for almost a month before returning to Mountainair. By that time the doctor had moved elsewhere, as he felt it was best to not encounter Shaffer again.

Shaffer explained his reasons for wanting to kill the doctor, *"The doctor gave Pearl medicine for a bad cold she caught, but by the 20th of February she had to stay in bed and remained there until she died. After she got so bad she couldn't go into town, I would try to get the doctor to come out to see her, but he wouldn't. He would send medicine for her out by me, but she kept getting worse all the time. I would see him every day and kept asking him to come out, but all he would do was send medicine and say she would be alright."*

Pop Shaffer was heart-broken over the death of Pearl. He had always been a drinking man, but his friends worried about his drinking after his wife's death. He later wrote about the experience, "After Pearl's funeral I stayed in Indiana for about three weeks and left my children with their grandparents, Ma and Pa Brown."

He returned to Mountainair to pick up the pieces of his life and continued in the real estate and blacksmith business. But, a year after Pearl's death, he decided to marry Lena Imboden. The two had known one another for years and Pop was a good friend of Lena's father who everyone in the community referred to as Dad Imboden. He was a generous man who helped many of the homesteaders in the area and his daughter reacted in the same manner.

POP SHAFFER IN THE 1920s

****

Lena homesteaded her own land near Dad Imboden's homestead and had fallen in love with a local boy she planned on marrying. Unfortunately, he died during an influenza epidemic leaving her in mourning. So, in the beginning she was not interested in marrying Shaffer and would only dance with him at one of the many country dances held during those years. Their union was one of convenience especially in the beginning of their marriage. But, they would learn to care for one another and spent the remainder of their lives together.

Lena had always wanted to operate a hotel and restaurant, so when Clem's blacksmith shop burned to the ground in 1922, the couple decided to erect a restaurant and hotel in its place. Shaffer was determined to make sure his newest business would remain standing and made the hotel of concrete reinforced with iron scraps from the blacksmith shop. The hotel would open for business in 1924.

From the beginning, Lena placed her own signature on the hotel and worked hard to make it a place people wanted to visit. Ernie Pyle described Lena in a 1942 interview, "She is good humored and works herself practically to death. She helps cook and waits on tables and acts as a room clerk." She stated to Pyle, "They keep piling more work on me all the time. The other day they added two hours, so now I'm working 26 hours a day."

Lena was excited about the prospect of running a hotel and she put all of her love and devotion into making it a homey place for those needing a place to stay while on the road. She prepared homemade meals and told stories about the settlement of the country. She was loved and appreciated by visitors and locals dining at the restaurant. Many people returned and stayed at the hotel again and again because of Lena's hospitality.

SHAFFER HOTEL SHORTLY AFTER CONSTRUCTION

Shaffer explained his reasons for building the Hotel Shaffer, "*In 1923 my blacksmith shop burned down so I started to build a new concrete building for a hardware store and implement house. I got the first story up and the traveling men got after me to put in a second floor on top of the concrete and put a hotel up there. My wife heard them talking to me about it and she wanted me to do that. She said, I'll run it, so she is still running it."*

The hotel business was quite successful and Shaffer decided to build an addition to the east of the building in 1929. He began to paint the interior of the hotel in 1931 using many of the skills he had learned while working as a carriage and buggy painter in Oklahoma. The dining room ceiling is mesmerizing and shows a little of Clem Shaffer's personality. He is often touted as the first artist in Mountainair.

SHAFFER HOTEL
DINING ROOM

Pop was not one to obey the rules and those in law enforcement did not always make him comply with the ordinances in town. Mountainair made it illegal to sell liquor within the town limits, yet Pop was allowed to operate a drinking establishment between the Shaffer and the railroad depot that flourished for decades before he became tired of running it and went on to another adventure.

Shaffer was extremely patriotic and occasionally boarded a train in Mountainair bound either for Los Angeles or Chicago. Ernie Pyle added, *"He never bothered to tell his wife he was going anywhere; the local railroad agent was the only person in town who knew for certain where Pop was. Upon his arrival in these cities, he sought out soldiers—men in uniform. He bought them dinner and drinks until his money ran out. He stayed out all night partying with the soldiers sometimes spending as much as $200.00."*

Pop was always involved in some business deal and said to be handy with tools. When he first arrived in Mountainair he purchased old broken down wagons for a dollar. He then repaired and painted them and sold them for $75.00. Everyone needed a wagon in those days, and they knew Pop's renovations would be good work as he never did anything half way.

Pop found a house in the country and moved it next to the hotel for his family to live in. The house was later lost to fire and the Shaffer family moved back into the hotel.

CLEM SHAFFER'S BLACKSMITH SHOP

Pop was also an early real estate agent and commented he had once bought and sold most of the land around Mountainair and still owned half of the buildings in town. When Shaffer was thirty-seven years old, he decided to retire from his many business ventures in Mountainair and concentrate on Rancho Bonito and his passion for creating unusual animal art. He stated in an interview with Ernie Pyle, "I turned the hotel over to Lena in order to get it off my hands," he said while standing in front of her. "She knows she's gotta do it or I'll quit. I'll go out to Los Angeles and get me one of those redheads with lots of money. Somebody's got to keep me up."

The hotel's restaurant was successful because of Lena Shaffer. She did most of the cooking and cleaning and served T-bone steaks for 50 cents and two eggs cooked anyway for 15 cents. The menu also listed a family style daily special at 65 cents for adults, 40 cents for children. The house bargain no doubt was the Special Bean Dinner—pintos, bread, butter and coffee for 15 cents.

Many people in Mountainair felt Lena may have been too tolerant of Clem, as he had a partying side to him she could not always control. He often went to Albuquerque or other cities in the state where he drank with friends and spent several days at a time. There are rumors that he was involved with a red head from out of town that he spent a good deal of his time with. Many referred to her as his mistress.

One story tells that when Lena was shopping for supplies for the restaurant, Pop would invite his mistress to the hotel. One morning when Lena returned earlier than usual she caught her husband climbing the stairs with a red-haired woman. Lena drew her pistol as did Shaffer's mistress. They both took a shot at one another at the same time, but both were wide of their marks. Lena's bullet hit the ceiling behind the staircase. The other woman's bullet lodged in the molding of the ceiling opposite the staircase.

This story has been repeated many times throughout the hotel's history but no real proof has ever been provided for the verification of this incident. Pop Shaffer was also reported to shoot into the ceiling of the lobby when he drank to excess. A few stories state Lena wrestled the gun away from Pop on several occasions. Maybe it really happened or maybe it was a good story to lure tourists to the hotel for the weekend.

Pop Shaffer also liked to tell "tall tales" to the tourists passing through and many stopped at the Shaffer Hotel hoping they would get the chance to visit with him. He was known throughout New Mexico and the Southwest in the 1930s and 1940s and many made weekend vacation plans that included spending the night at the Shaffer Hotel. Shaffer also placed quirky advertisements in local magazines and publications. He was ahead of his time in many ways and had a shrewd mind for advertising. He wanted to make the hotel one of the most unusual in the region, and it seems he accomplished his goal. The old hotel contains many interesting artifacts he left behind.

**PHOTO BELIEVED TO BE
LENA IMBODEN SHAFFER**

Pop made frequent trips to California. He returned with photos of himself and attractive women. Of course Lena did not approve, but Clem generally did things his own way. She stayed busy at the hotel, her rose garden, crocheting, canning and making big yellow bars of laundry soap. She also took and developed photographs for the public and found contentment in running the premiere hotel in Torrance County and visiting with her family and friends.

Pop stated in an interview with Ernie Pyle that on these trips he often registered in one hotel room and ended up in another. Shaffer was unable to complete an entire sentence without cussing. He was popular among the people of Mountainair. One story goes that for a time he had the local coffin business in town. When he drank too much and passed out his friends put him in his best suit and placed him inside the coffin. Everyone had a good laugh when he woke up the next morning, but his friends said he did not drink for a year after the prank. Lena even had to lock him up in a downstairs room when he got out of control with the guests after drinking too much and would not calm down for the evening. Shaffer enjoyed drinking a little too much at times.

Pyle also wrote, *"And Pop has fun too. He likes to put on a fling-ding every once in awhile. He'll go to Albuquerque and party. He's also gone to Hollywood on more than one occasion where he frequented the night clubs and had his photo taken with the cuties, then brought them home."*

SWASTIKAS ON FRONT OF SHAFFER HOTEL

Today when people see the Shaffer Hotel, they wonder why Clem Shaffer decorated the front with swastikas. Pop painted the swastikas on the front of the hotel over twenty years before Adolph Hitler made the symbol a source of hate. It had long been used as a Navajo peace symbol. Shaffer meant it in this manner, and in later years after World War II, people asked Clem why he didn't paint over the swastikas on the front of the hotel. He replied that he would not replace the symbols. It was not his fault a ruler over in distant Europe decided to go crazy.

One interpretation of the swastika is a Native American symbol called "Rolling Logs" meaning the four corners of the earth, the four seasons, and the four elements, all coming together in love and harmony. It seems to be used most often in the Navajo culture.

Shaffer used the swastika symbol as a symbol of good luck and peace for all his guests and friends who frequented the hotel. The swastika symbol was quite prevalent in New Mexico. Hotels, newspapers, Albuquerque's Kimo Theater all used the symbol, as did, businesses, schools and even theater companies. It had a completely different meaning during Shaffer's time.

In 1937 the Indian National met and vowed never to use the symbol again because Hitler changed it from a symbol of love to a symbol of hate. In the past century, it has reverted to the evil symbol left by Hitler's regime. Pop liked the way the symbol dressed up the front of his hotel and attracted visitors.

The swastikas remain on the front of the hotel and are often a topic for conversation among those visiting the town and hotel. Shaffer often discussed Native American lore with those visiting Rancho Bonito and the Shaffer Hotel, and the swastikas were a good point to start his discussion of the hotel when visitors stopped by.

**CLEM SHAFFER AND HIS UNIQUE WALL
WEST OF THE HOTEL**

**SHAFFER'S WALL & HOUSE THAT WAS
LOST TO FIRE**

SHAFFER'S WALL

INSIDE SHAFFER HOTEL 1920s

Clem Shaffer passed away at Albuquerque's Bataan Hospital after suffering a heart attack on November 25, 1964. He was eighty-four years old. Lena, who outlived Clem by 14 years, finally closed the old hotel in 1970.

Dixie Reid wrote an article in the Albuquerque Journal in June of 1984 about Shaffer. She wrote, *"Pop Shaffer is buried on a hill overlooking Mountainair, but his grave sits with its simple gray granite marker planted among dry, blowing weeds isn't right. Not for him anyway. Nothing there reflects the whimsy of Pop Shaffer—not the two empty mayonnaise jars and red coffee can that someone painted in the crusty mound over his body, not the sun-bleached red plastic roses scattered about the dry, cracked ground, not the single Iris at his feet. Even the tombstone inscription—Clem Shaffer—is wrong. Everyone called him Pop."*

****

Countless stories have been written about Pop Shaffer, the Shaffer Hotel, and Rancho Bonito, Shaffer's folk art style ranch south of Mountainair. Yet, the contributions of his wife Lena Shaffer have been largely overlooked or briefly mentioned. She was not only in agreement with her husband to construct the hotel but volunteered to run it as well. It was largely due to Lena Shaffer's innovative ideas, friendly personality, and hard work that the Shaffer Hotel and its dining room became a popular destination for those looking for food and lodging during Mountainair's early years.

Lena Shaffer was born Lena Imboden in Missouri in 1892, but her family moved soon afterwards to a homestead near Bloom, Kansas where she spent her childhood. By 1900, the Imboden family had moved to a homestead six miles north of Mountainair and settled into a life of pinto bean farming during the boom years when Mountainair was known as the Pinto Bean Capital of the World. Lena, later filed on her own homestead, where she lived alone for part of the year in order to receive legal claim to the land.

During her younger years, Lena was known as a "country belle" and had more than one young man interested in marrying her. When her fiancée passed away during an influenza epidemic she was broken hearted. A year later, she and Clem started to court. At first, they would meet at one of the local dances held each week in Mountainair or at one of the surrounding towns. Later, the couple was seen taking buggy rides on Sunday afternoons.

They were married in July of 1912 and had one son named Martin the following year. Martin would go on to become a well-known professional artist, who settled in Taos and opened Shaffer Studios there in the 1940s. Clem Shaffer was often heard to say that Lena was the best mother he could have ever found for all of his children.

Most sources give Clem credit for the success of the Shaffer Hotel but in reality Lena made the business successful. To make extra money after dinner had been served, Lena rented out the dining room, including the piano and phonograph, for $2.00 a night. Many times, musicians staying at the hotel played for the guests. The most famous musician to play for the group was Harmon Nelson, Jr., actress Bette Davis' first husband and high school sweetheart. He stopped at the hotel in 1930 while on his way to Boston to marry Davis. Lena Shaffer prepared breakfast for this group in the wee hours of the morning. The establishment became so popular at times that if guests did not arrive early, they had to find lodging elsewhere.

Ernie Pyle left an interesting quote about Pop Shaffer. He wrote, *"When Pop arrived in Mountainair this town was just opening up. Pop Shaffer homesteaded, he blacksmithed, he ran a hardware store, he contracted and in 1923 he built a hotel. He still has his first two dollars he took in—silver dollars tacked up on the wall."*

Shaffer was definitely a hard working man who did things in his own manner. His historic hotel was a necessary addition to the town of Mountainair and helped it to grow and prosper in the early years. Lena worked harder than Clem and was loved and respected by the community.

Lena Shaffer's contributions to the history of the hotel have been largely overlooked. She most definitely deserves the credit for the success and management of Mountainair's Shaffer Hotel. Not only was she loyal to her wandering husband in spite of his vices, she was also dedicated to running a top-notch hotel and ensuring the satisfaction of her guests. She was constantly busy and fondly remembered by those who knew her. She was not one to complain and was always willing to lend a hand or make the hotel and café more inviting for guests. In many ways, Lena was obsessed with working and worked long after the hotel and restaurant had closed for the evening.

Lena lived in the hotel alone for the last eight years of her life. She continued to work in her flower garden and walk to the grocery store when she needed supplies. Her many friends checked on her throughout the week.

A. T. & S. Fe Depot, Mountainair, N. Mex.

MOUNTAINAIR DEPOT

CHAPTER TWO – RANCHO BONITO

POP SHAFFER'S LOG CABIN

Rancho Bonito, Pop Shaffer's unusual folk-style ranch, is located a few miles south of Mountainair. He came into possession of the 240 acres making up the property when a local farmer could not pay his delinquent taxes. He made the location into his art studio and getaway where he also entertained tourists and visitors as well as local residents.

Rancho Bonito was not only Shaffer's getaway and art studio, but it served a practical purpose as well. Shaffer cultivated a large garden and orchard on the site and raised chickens and cows to provide the hotel with fresh vegetables, eggs, milk, cream and butter. Chicken and steaks were also part of the menu at the Shaffer Restaurant when Shaffer had extra on the farm.

For years a stone monument was located near the front gate. It was a patriotic plague on which George Washington, Abraham Lincoln and Teddy Roosevelt's profiles were reproduced in sandstone. Teddy's eye glasses were flat round rocks. Many visitors of the time drove by in order to see the monument and take pictures.

The famous WWII war correspondent, Ernie Pyle wrote about Shaffer's Rancho Bonito in the *Albuquerque Journal*, *"Pop's Rancho Bonito is a sight . . . There are many buildings, including a crazy house for his tenants, a showroom for his smaller pieces of animal art, a barn and a chicken house. Most of the ranch buildings are of stone, and everything is inlaid with rock pictures of everything from Uncle Sam to a cross-eyed owl. And the whole ranch is wildly colored like a carnival."*

The entire piece of property became a showcase for Shaffer's artwork, and he was constantly walking through the woods looking for unusual pieces of wood to make into pieces of art. The many people visiting Rancho Bonito were impressed with Shaffer's artwork and often had their photographs taken in front of one piece or another.

Pop Shaffer began a tradition in Mountainair for artist-types seeking free expression and individuality. He converted Rancho Bonito into a place for him to work on his animal artwork. He is known as an American Folk Environmentalist, an artist who shares no direct relationship with the art of the past or awareness of developments of the art of their contemporaries. They work outside the mainstream, intently focusing on an inner vision, the content, scope, and style of which is the sole product of the artist.

POP SHAFFER WORKING ON HIS ART

Shaffer possessed an obsession of sorts for creating works of art out of twisted pieces of wood. He was a productive artist and once vowed he would create one thousand of his "critters" before he died. The cabin at Rancho Bonito was covered with his artwork, inside and out. People stopped from all over the country to see his unique style of artwork. But, Lena sold most of his artwork to *The Thing,* a roadside attraction on the Arizona and Nevada border. She was heard to say, more than once, that she did not appreciate his artwork as much as the rest of the people.

In 1942, Shaffer traveled to Washington, D.C. taking 45 of his wooden sculptures with the intention of having them exhibited in the National Art Week Exhibit sponsored by the White House. When he arrived, he was told he could not exhibit his artwork without prior approval. He pleaded and begged but no one was interested in listening to him.

He was pacing the hallway wondering how he could sneak a few pieces into the exhibit when Eleanor Roosevelt arrived for her official visit. He approached her and introduced himself and told her about his problem. She took his arm and they walked to the basement. She liked his artwork and insisted his "critters" be included in the exhibit. He gave the first lady a knitting stand made of wood and gourds that looked like a goose and the president received a wooden ashtray shaped like a monkey.

With all the publicity, many travelers visited Rancho Bonito, arriving by train in Mountainair or later by motorcar. According to visitation estimates, 12,000 people visited Rancho Bonito in a single year, mainly wanting to see Shaffer's creations. Hundreds stayed at the Shaffer Hotel. Pop Shaffer's Rancho Bonito became known for its crazy wooden critters especially in the 1940s. Shaffer had a sense of humor and told stories in an engaging manner. Many felt it was due to Clem Shaffer and the tourist business that Mountainair survived when the growing of pinto beans went bust.

ONE OF SHAFFER'S CREATIONS

Many of the tourists passing through stopped in order to look at Rancho Bonito and Shaffer's "critters." Shaffer also provided accommodations for those wanting to stay and they could have breakfast at the hotel the following morning. Many moved away when they could no longer grow pinto beans but Pop Shaffer was not one to give up and capitalized on the tourist trade.

Shaffer being extremely patriotic used red, white and blue in the color scheme at Rancho Bonito. First, he built a barn that looked like a Swiss Chalet. Next, he constructed a one-room cabin and painted it red, white and blue—inside and out. Even the windows, no two the same size were half clear panes and half stained glass. Pop never lived at Rancho Bonito but he went there daily. It was his art studio, a place to have fun and also a place where he could get away from it all.

Pop Shaffer had an interesting personality as reflected in his artwork. He was able to see images in pieces of wood that no one could see until the piece was completed. He spent hours walking through the woods looking for interesting pieces of wood in which to create his "critters." His workshop at Rancho Bonito was the perfect location to work on his creations, and he spent endless happy hours making his wooden images.

**ONE OF SHAFFER'S "CRITTERS" STILL
ADORNS THE GATE AT RANCHO BONITO**

STONE COTTAGE AT
RANCHO BONITO

Shaffer's Rancho Bonito attracted a record number of visitors in the 1930s and 1940s. Some came to fish in the pond he dug next to the cabin. He mainly dug the pond and stocked it with fish to fulfill his own need to fish. In later years, he broke glass and placed in the bottom of the pond to keep the local kids from sneaking in when he was not there and skinny dipping. He was afraid one of the kids might drown.

Another quote from Ernie Pyle shows how much Pop enjoyed fishing, *"Pop loves to fish; loves it so much he has built a lake at the ranch. It isn't much bigger than a barn, yet Pop has a rowboat and rows out in the middle of it and fishes. He doesn't depend on nature for worms either. For this arid land dries them up so hard in the summer you couldn't find an earthworm with a witching stick. So in the barn he has five washtubs of moistened earth and this earth is alive with fish worms."*

TOURISTS VISITING RANCHO BONITO
IN THE 1940s

Rancho Bonito was placed on the National Register of Historic Places in 1978. Included in the Register were five buildings and fourteen acres. All the structures were built in the 1930s.

Dorothy Cole purchased Rancho Bonito from the Shaffer family in 1990 and did the first major restoration on the property. She converted the stone house into her living quarters. When she first moved in the residence had electricity but no running water. The stone house was designed and built of local materials by Pop Shaffer.

She did the restoration work herself and gave tours and worked to preserve the history of Rancho Bonito. Cole knew Pop Shaffer personally and recounted interesting stories about his life and character when visitors stopped to view the unique folk art style ranch he had created.

Dorothy naturally assumed the role of town historian when she returned to her home town of Mountainair. She gave historical lectures and musical concerts and took care of Rancho Bonito. Pop Shaffer himself could not have found a better caretaker than Dorothy Cole.

Nick and Francesca Romero purchased the property from Dorothy Cole in 2016. They have painted and upgraded the property. Before Cole passed away, she searched for someone who would love and care for the property as she and Pop Shaffer had done beforehand. She felt Nick and Francesca would be good caretakers at Rancho Bonito.

Rancho Bonito is NOT open to the public, but visitors can drive by and see Shaffer's unique gate and buildings from the road.

MOUNTAINAIR DEPOT

CHAPTER THREE-- PARANORMAL ACTIVITY AT THE SHAFFER HOTEL

SHAFFER HOTEL IN THE 1980s

There are those who believe the Shaffer Hotel is haunted. Visitors have reported seeing lights flash on and off in the middle of the night accompanied by strange laughter and later those staying the night noticed items had been moved in their rooms. Several felt they were being watched and could not go to sleep at night while others noticed an eerie shadow or two at the end of the dark hallway. At other times, the elevator moved up and down and there was no one on it. Even, distinct footsteps echoed in the hallway late at night, yet when someone investigated no one was there.

On other occasions, visitors noticed window blinds moving in some rooms while others heard a female voice humming or singing. At times, the pool cues were heard falling to the ground in the game room and guests heard the water being turned on and off. The smell of chocolate permeated the west wing a good part of the time and more than one guest heard the sound of happy children's voices.

Additional ghostly images have been reported: One was an apparition of a large woman with a yellow and red face who may have worked in a carnival. Pop Shaffer often invited a carnival to set up nearby during the Fourth of July and other holidays, and one story has survived about two carnival workers having a terrible fight one evening after the carnival closed. They were beating one another with chains. Visitors at the hotel were often approached by the ghost of a woman asking them in a desperate voice to please help her stop the fight, as she was afraid the two men would kill one another.

Another ghost reported by those working at the hotel, was of a woman who worked in the kitchen as a cook. She was heard banging pans and someone humming a happy tune. Another ghost was that of a pale, young girl who many say was murdered. Some have heard her terrified screams near the back door of the kitchen while others reported screams in the alleyway behind the hotel.

Eerie noises are heard throughout the old hotel especially when it settles down for the evening. From time to time, a thumping sound is heard from above in the east wing, where many believe a young cowboy hung himself when his fiancée married someone else. Gunshots and Pop Shaffer's drunken laughter echo throughout the old hotel lobby on full-moon nights, as well as, the sound of two women yelling at one another and loud gunshots, screaming and insane laughter.

The hotel's former proprietors Clem and Lena Shaffer are the two ghosts sighted the most often at the old hotel. More than one person has reported seeing Lena standing in the hallway upstairs or passing through the kitchen. Glimpses of a woman fitting Lena's description appear west of the hotel at times in her former rose and flower garden. She is always humming a melancholy tune no one can understand.

During the many years the hotel was vacant, a dark shadow was seen going from one upstairs window to another. Many believe it was the ghost of Pop Shaffer who probably loved the old hotel more than anyone else except for Lena and still returns to make sure it's secure for the evening as he did when he was alive.

In later years, several visitors stated they had ghostly encounters while staying at the hotel. One of these encounters was recorded in John Mulhouse's *City of Dust Column* that tells about a family that spent an uncomfortable night at the hotel.

One Halloween night a father had requested that he and his daughters be given the most haunted room in the hotel. The man was put in 16, where the cowboy was said to have hung himself and his daughters got the adjoining room of the suite. In the middle of the night the man went to use the bathroom and felt a chill then turned to see the outline of a body on the bed. When he approached the bed, something threw him against the wall and he could not move. He attempted to go to his daughters but was unable to unlock the door to their room. Hearing the scuffle next door, his daughters awoke and discovered they were unable to unlock the door from their side either. Early the next morning the woman that runs the front desk came to find the man and his daughters sitting downstairs. The girls were crying. The man said they weren't staying another night and the hotel could keep their money as far as he was concerned. The clerk refunded their money anyway and apologized for their terrifying experience.

Another visitor reported meeting Pop Shaffer after he passed away. The visitor and her husband stopped by the Shaffer Hotel to take photos and check out Shaffer's unusual wall west of the hotel. While there a slim man approached them and told them the hotel belonged to him and explained some of its history. He also invited them to join him at Rancho Bonito where they were welcome to stay a few days. At the time, she thought she had encountered a crazy, old man but later saw a photo of Pop Shaffer and realized he was the one she had met. She was disappointed she had not taken him up on his offer to spend the night at Rancho Bonito.

In the late 1990s a waitress at the Shaffer heard the sound of someone wearing heavy boots behind her in the kitchen but when she turned to see who it was no one was there. The cook stated they were the only ones at the hotel, and she never left the kitchen area because she did not want to run into one of the ghosts said to haunt the old hotel.

The same waitress was in the restroom one night after closing. She heard the bathroom door open and the distinct sound of a woman sighing, as though she was frustrated, and then the door shut.

When she asked the cook if she had opened the restroom door, she replied she had been in the kitchen the entire time. They quickly locked up leaving the hotel with its ghosts for the evening. Both women saw the shadow of a woman standing at the back door as they drove away.

Over the years, guests staying in the haunted east wing have heard the sound of wagons and running water from the street below. Others were awakened by men's voices, horses neighing and the sound of endless wagons approaching and leaving. But, when they were brave enough to get up and look out the window, there was never anyone or anything there. Pop Shaffer also sold water from a well east of the Shaffer to pinto bean farmers in the area, especially those who lived south of Mountainair and did not have good water. He would greet them when they arrived in town, and even gave away free water when settlers first arrived in the area and had not had time to drill their own wells.

During the years the old hotel remained abandoned, music was heard on occasion by those living nearby or passing by the hotel especially on a Saturday night. Dancers from another era were even noticed having a good time through the lobby window but when someone investigated further, they had disappeared and only shadows remained as the music became more and more faint and eventually faded away. At other times, music from an old phonograph was heard echoing outside the building and the sound of laughter and happy voices. Saturday night dances were once a popular activity in Mountainair during the early years.

Those spending the night in the hotel's east wing have reported being awakened in the early hours of the morning by the sound and smell of a steam engine stopping at the nearby railroad depot. They noticed lights at the old depot and heard the sound of voices as people getting on and off the train greeted one another. A little later, they heard the sound of tramping feet in the hallway and doors opening and closing as the ghostly visitors settled into their rooms for the evening.

The following morning they discovered they had been the only ones staying in the hotel's east wing for the evening. When they asked the hotel clerk about the sounds in the night, she explained the old railroad depot had not been in service for close to forty years and steam engines had been obsolete for almost a century. She also explained that several other visitors to the hotel have heard similar sounds in the hallway after hearing a steam engine pass by on the railroad tracks. Pop Shaffer's old hotel was quite active during the days when the railroad depot remained open and people used it as a major means of travel. Those riding the train often walked the two blocks from the railroad depot to the hotel after getting off the train. They were greeted by both Clem and Lena Shaffer when they arrived at the hotel and usually there was dancing and other activities for those staying at the hotel for the night.

MOUNTAINAIR'S RAILROAD DEPOT
1919

After the elevator was installed in the hotel, it seemed a playful ghost enjoyed riding it up and down and opening and closing the doors at all hours of the day and night. Many believe it is the ghost of Pop Shaffer. John Cates, one of the first managers under Joel Marks' tenure stated there was usually a lot of activity at night at the hotel. When the guests settled down for the evening, the sounds would echo through the hotel. Banging sounds were heard, plus people talking, arguing and laughing in the hallways and below in the hotel dining room.

In an interview in *New Mexico Magazine* in May of 2006, former owner Joel Marks explained the forms of ghostly activity at the hotel. He stated, "There's definitely an "energy" here, especially in the east wing, which is over the painted ceiling of the restaurant. But it's not a bad energy maybe Pop is just still having fun here."

Late one evening in the 1940s, a woman's vehicle stalled on the railroad tracks not far from the hotel. She was struggling to get her children out of the car when they were hit by a train. In the years following the accident, people driving over the railroad tracks during the evening hours often encountered the woman. She would try and stop them and begged for help to save her children. She was seen searching and heard wailing for her lost children along the tracks especially when the moon was full. Many referred to her as the *La Llorona* and still believe she roams the tracks late at night desperately searching for her children.

Artists Linda Carol and Rebecca Anthony opened La Galeria in the Shaffer Hotel in the spring of 2019. One evening, they noticed an alarm had gone off in the art gallery and it appeared someone was trying to break into the building. They were both home at the time and rushed to the Shaffer Hotel but upon their arrival there appeared to be nothing wrong or out of place. The only item they discovered was a painting that had popped out of its frame and was on the floor.

LA GALERIA ART GALLERY
SHAFFER HOTEL

When they took a look at the security camera, all they saw were orb like shapes on the camera but no other movement. Yet, the painting of the red-haired woman was found on the floor several more times before finally remaining on the wall where it had been placed. Maybe the ghost of Lena put the painting on the floor because she did not want to be reminded of the red-haired mistress her husband had once spent so much time with. Or maybe the wind rocked the painting to the floor before it was firmly secured to the wall. Another time, the door to the gallery opened on its own several times when there was no breeze or activity. Lena Shaffer was probably letting the managers of the Galeria know she would like the painting removed.

MOUNTAINAIR DEPOT CIRCA 1940s

CHAPTER FOUR – OWNERS & MANAGERS OF THE SHAFFER HOTEL

Lena Shaffer operated the Shaffer Hotel between the years of 1923 and 1970. She had to close the hotel dining room in 1943 because most of her help went off to fight in WWII. She never reopened the dining room but leased it to others and continued renting rooms in the hotel until 1970. After retiring from the hotel business, she continued to live in the Shaffer Hotel until her death in 1978. The Calderon family operated the dining room in the 1970s and rooms were occasionally rented in the hotel, yet business was not what it had been earlier in the century.

**SHAFFER HOTEL IN
THE 1970s**

There have been numerous managers of the hotel and restaurant over the years. Most leased the building with the option to buy but never actually received clear title to the property.

Other than the Shaffer family, it appears the hotel has had only a few owners throughout its almost 100 year history. Harding Kayser and Joe J Brazil purchased the property in 1981, Dee Tarr was part owner of the business in the 1990s, the Bank of Belen owned the property for a number of years, antique dealer James Hecker purchased the hotel in 2002 and continues to own the property while in 2019 Ed VonKuteleben and his family took over the management of the business.

In the 1980s, the hotel had become run down, and Kayser and Brazil wanted to revert it to its former glory. They sought grants to cover the price of restoration and being carpenters began the first major restoration project on the first floor of the hotel which was desperately needed. Harding and Brazil had grown up in the area and been childhood friends. They had seen the hotel when it was in its prime and wanted to make it an integral part of the community once again.

After graduating from Mountainair High School, Kayser spent 25 years in the Navy before returning to Mountainair and selling real estate. He was a major promoter of Mountainair and is responsible for making Mountainair into the "Gateway to Ancient Cities," in an attempt to corral the tourist trade. Kayser served as the mayor of Mountainair from 1974-1978 and did much to improve the town. He passed away in 1995.

Joe J Brazil was born and raised in Scholle, a once booming railroad community west of Mountainair. Referred to as a poet and philosopher, he was also an accomplished artist. While serving in the South Pacific during WWII, he made enough money drawing portraits of his fellow soldiers and painting on B-24 bomber planes to start his first cattle herd when he returned home. He continued drawing in his spare time, and became an accomplished artist of ranch scenes and Western life. He died at his home outside Scholle in 2006.

In 1981, the newly organized Salinas Pueblo Missions National Monument made the Shaffer Hotel its headquarters. During this time, the building received further upgrades for a visitor center and offices. An elevator was installed in the lobby, and the old hotel was active once again. During this decade Herman and Leah Marie Riley managed the restaurant and changed the name of the dining room to the Pueblo Café.

Diedra Tarr was part owner and managed the hotel and restaurant from 1991 until 1996. She lived in the hotel for two years. During Tarr's tenure as manager the hotel did a bustling business. The business had a gift shop and art gallery during these years. There were often weddings, family reunions and other events at the hotel. Tarr stated that she worked 22 hours a day during these years keeping up with her responsibilities. She enjoyed the experience very much and has fond memories of her time at the Shaffer Hotel.

Albuquerque native Joel Marks leased to own the building starting in 2004. He began the first extensive restoration project on the hotel which reportedly cost a million dollars by the time it was completed.

He cut down the original 30 guest rooms to 19 and replaced many of the rooms with private baths. The hotel opened once again under Mark's management in 2005.

Mark's was riding his Harley-Davidson motorcycle through the Manzano Mountains one afternoon and stopped at the Shaffer Hotel for lunch. As most visitors to the hotel, he was awed by the atmosphere of the hotel and the Pueblo Deco ceiling Shaffer had created. When the hotel came up for sale a few weeks later, he decided to purchase the business and begin a major restoration project on the old building.

Marks' leased the hotel for fifteen years and many managers served during his time at the hotel. The first managers were John and Karen Cate and their pet parrot Eclectus from Sedona, Arizona. They were managing a $20 million dollar Best Western on the Navajo Reservation when they saw an advertisement on the Internet looking for innkeepers in Mountainair.

They were ready for a different opportunity and decided to move to Mountainair and manage the Shaffer Hotel. John stated in an interview online, "We got to Mountainair in April of 2005. Joel had poured more than half a million dollars into the renovation of the rooms upstairs that I oversaw."

The hotel went through one manager after another for a decade, before Jerry and Alma Pack took over the management of the property in 2011. They established a popular catfish dinner on Friday nights and sponsored different musicians and performances to attract customers.

The hotel continued to operate on an intermittent basis until the spring of 2019 when VonKuteleben assumed control of the business. Those living in Mountainair and throughout New

Mexico, hope the hotel remains open and continues to prosper. In many ways it serves as a museum of Mountainair's past.

**BUSINESS CAR IN MOUNTAINAIR
CIRCA 1960s**

CONCLUSION

PRESENT DAY
SHAFFER HOTEL

For close to a century the Shaffer Hotel has watched the history of Mountainair go from boom to bust and gradually back again. During Mountainair's heyday years in the 1920s and 1930s, the town boasted a population of 3,000 people. In the most current census, the town's population had dropped to a thousand. Yet, Mountainair continues to prosper more than other small towns along the Belen Cutoff railroad route.

When the Santa Fe Railroad decided to downsize in the 1940s and 1960s, it closed its depots in half of the towns along the route. The towns had grown up around the depots and when they were closed, many began to decline and lose population. The depots were either moved and used somewhere else or demolished. Mountainair's depot remained open until the late 1960s and has been used by the railroad for office space and storage since.

There were also three Harvey Houses along the Belen Cutoff Route: the Gran Quivira in Clovis, the Los Chavez in Vaughn and the Belen Harvey House in Belen. The Belen Harvey House now serves as a museum and has been renovated and restored. Yet, the downsizing of the railroad would hurt the economy of the railroad towns it had created over a century earlier. Mountainair would be no exception and the economy of the town suffered in the 1970s and 1980s.

During Mountainair's early years, the street in front of the Shaffer Hotel served as the town's main street. The railroad depot was located at the east end of the street and there was always a lot of activity between the depot and the Shaffer Hotel. The train was the most popular means of transportation during the early years of the twentieth century.

Most of the buildings between the Shaffer Hotel and railroad depot have been lost to fire and razing over the years. The Farr and Shockey bean elevators remain as a reminder of the town's founding and farming past.

FARR BEAN ELEVATOR

Many residents of Mountainair remember when the depot was open. Yet, now this section of town is often quiet. The echo of the train passing through is only a vague reminder of the town's more active past. Fortunately, the Shaffer Hotel is once again open. People can visit, enjoy and learn about the history of the town and people when the train was the main form of transportation and the Shaffer Hotel a destination along the route.

The establishment of railroad lines throughout the country and especially in the western states was actively sought during the years before and after the turn of the twentieth century. Everyone wanted the railroad to come through the section of the country or state where they were living, as it usually caused a boom to the economy. It also provided a quicker means of transportation when traveling to nearby towns. In addition the railroad depots were a place to meet and visit with neighbors and friends while watching the trains pass by.

Hotels and eating establishments were constructed near the railroad tracks in most frontier communities. They were often the first businesses in town and from there these early communities along the tracks began to grow and prosper as town's developed nearby.

The Shaffer Hotel has watched Mountainair grow from a raw railroad town along the Belen Cut-Off to the Pinto Bean Capital of the World. The old hotel watched the town come close to extinction before "making a comeback" as a tourist, artist and retiree community where visitors can learn about the history of the area and camp and recreate in the nearby Manzano Mountains.

MOUNTAINAIR PHOTO ALBUM

MOUNTAINAIR HOSPITAL

**WILLARD MERCANTILE COMPANY
LATER MOUNTAINAIR TRADING COMPANY
& LAWSON'S STORE**

FIRST SCHOOL IN MOUNTAINAIR
REFERRED TO AS THE VEAL DUGOUT

ORIGINAL MOUNTAINAIR
HIGH SCHOOL

LA GRAN QUIVIRA CURIO SHOP NOW
SERVES AS TOBY'S TIRE SHOP NEXT TO THE
MUSTANG DINER

**CHISUM'S BARBER POLE
MOUNTAINAIR MOTOR COMPANY IN
BACKGROUND**

TRINIDAD BEAN ELEVATOR

J J WHITE MERCHANDISE STORE
EAST END OF MOUNTAINAIR

MOUNTAINAIR REALTY COMPANY
CIRCA 1909

WOMACK GENERAL MERCHANDISE
LATER UNCLE WALTER'S AND THE
EMPORIUM

ARROW FILLING STATION

**MOUNTAINAIR TELEPHONE
COMPANY**

GOLDEN GRILL CAFÉ
BETWEEN GUSTIN'S HARDWARE &
GYPSY'S

)N'S MOUNTAINAIR MOTEL – "Nature Cooled" – U. S. Hwy 60 East in Mountainair, N. M.

NELSON'S MOUNTAINAIR MOTEL
NOW TURNER'S INN

**MOUNTAINAIR'S PINTO BEAN PARADE
IN 1941**

**MOUNTAINAIR BASEBALL TEAM
CIRCA 1930s**

WEAVER GARAGE

PAUL'S STORE & THE EL CHARRO RESTAURANT—PROPRIETOR CARMEN PADILLA

REFERENCES

Herrman, Bert. *Mountainair, NM Centennial History 1903-2003.* Mountainair Public Schools, NM, 2003.

Mulhouse, John. *City of Dust Blog.* January, 2002.

Larese, Steve. Shaffer Hotel State's Newest Oldest Hotel. *New Mexico Magazine,* May 2006.

Niederman, Sharon. Rancho Bonito A Folk-Art Home on the Range. *New Mexico Magazine,* April, 2002.

Perea, Carol. Owner Joel Marks Believes He was Drawn to Mountainair's Landmark Hotel. *Mountain View Telegraph.* January 23, 2006.

Pyle, Ernie. *Albuquerque Journal,* April, 1942.

Reid, Dixie. *Pop's Art. Albuquerque Journal,* June 1984.

Historical Shaffer Hotel Photos courtesy of Shaffer Hotel.

Personal interview with Rebecca Anthony, November 10, 2019.

Personal interview with Linda Carol, November 20, 2019.

Personal interview with Dee Tarr, December 9, 2019.

Personal Interview with Ed VonKuteleben, December 14, 2019.

Photo of author on back cover taken by Sheila David.

HAULING PINTO BEANS TO MOUNTAINAIR DEPOT CIRCA 1915

Made in the USA
Middletown, DE
20 June 2022

67436446R00054